Published by: Kainos Enterprises
                   7777 Churchville Road
                   Brampton Ontario Canada L6Y 0H3
                   www.kainos.org
All scripture quotations, unless otherwise indicated, are taken from the HOLY BIBLE, NEW INTERNATIONAL VERSION®. NIV®. Copyright ©1973, 1978, 1984, 2011 by International Bible Society. Used by permission of Zondervan. All rights reserved.
ISBN: 978-1497311701

Contents

Dedication

This book is dedicated to my ever faithful, loving husband Gary. For most of our married life I have been his proofreader and have done some light editing for his numerous writing projects. But in recent years he has been encouraging me to do my own writing. So here it is, however, I agree more and more with Winston Churchill's quote, "Writing a book is an adventure. To begin with, it is a toy and an amusement; then it becomes a mistress, and then it becomes a master, and then a tyrant. The last phase is that just as you are about to be reconciled to your servitude, you kill the monster, and fling him out to the public."

I also would like this book to be my legacy to our four children and their spouses – Sara & Chris, Rebekah & Jerome, Rob & Jessica and Lee & Melissa – and their children, our special grandchildren – Cassidy, Kaiya, Carleigh, Evan, Faith, Sydney, Ava, Jade, Isabella, Aiden and Sophia.

A big thank you to Rebekah for her bird and flower artwork and to her daughter, Faith, who drew the "bug" between chapters!

Introduction

A journalist once reported in our local newspaper, "There's nothing nicer than a summer stroll through Churchville." You might hear the tolling of church bells in the background plus all manner of birds in the foreground. If you are walking in the late evening you can listen to the yipping of coyotes that gather in the large field by the river.

My husband, Gary, and I love living in our little historic Canadian village of about 100 homes. Churchville is located inside the city of Brampton, Ontario (a suburb just northwest of Toronto) along the meandering Credit River. It is country in the city. Whenever a friend, delivery person, or repairman comes through our front door, the expression on their face is always the same – they seem dazed. It's as if this person has been transported down into the peaceful valley of this whole new world that mesmerizes their soul.

Churchville was first established in 1815, our house was built around 1837 and we purchased it in the fall of 2006. Our backyard had hardly any gardens with some landscaping done to the front of the house by the previous owner. We have a small two-storey outbuilding shaped like a barn at the end of the driveway where Gary has his office upstairs and a workshop downstairs. He enjoys looking over the beautiful field of flowers on our neighbors' property next door from his office window as they own a perennial nursery business surrounding our land. My parents died a few months after our move. Just before the sale of their Toronto residence we transported a lot of their greenery to our home. I cannot claim to be an expert gardener but I did learn a fair bit from my mom when she was alive. I also have gained added knowledge from my horticulturalist neighbor since living in Churchville. That knowledge provided me with further confidence in looking after outside decor. What a surprise when last summer Gary hastened me out to the front yard one Saturday morning to see the Brampton Horticultural Society Award sign sticking in the ground at the end of our walkway. I'm still chuckling over that. I guess I have grown a "green thumb" over the years but not because of working with tobacco. In early America farmers would hand-pick tobacco flowers using their thumbnails to cut the stem which would stain their thumbs green after time. (I just thought you might like to know where that idiom stemmed from!)

A few years ago my brother-in-law, Cam, gave us a Christmas gift of a bird feeder in the shape of a red barn. Gary stuck a spike in the ground ten feet from our kitchen window, added a post and placed the bird feeder on top of a 2 x 2 foot platform on the post. Within a year determined squirrels had demolished the feeder by badly gnawing the wood looking for seed inside so we had to throw it away. We kept the platform and since then have used it as a feeding station for all the birds (and the squirrels!) in the vicinity. On occasion these birds could use a bird air traffic controller as this spot has become quite popular. I have definitely learned lots about our feathered friends but again I am not an expert bird-watcher or ornithologist.

When Jesus was living on earth He taught His disciples about His wonderful creation. He urged them to "look at the birds" (Matthew 6:26; Luke 12:24) and "consider the lilies" (Matthew 6:28; Luke 12:27). That is what Gary and I have been doing from our kitchen window while we eat our meals during the various seasons

In short chapters I have tried to associate a bird with a flower that seems to have similar characteristics. As well I thoroughly believe the Bible is a great standard on how to live life to the fullest. I have tied each chapter with a related thought from one of its numerous pages of wisdom. I pray this devotional book will be an inspiration, an encouragement and an educator to you. As you look and consider anew bird and flower life intertwined with tidbits from our Churchville and family life reflections may it cause you to build up your own Christian and personal life in a better way. Our family of God is abundantly blessed as we grow through one generation after the other. Drop around some time for a cup of tea at our kitchen table or lounge in our gazebo for a bit behind our barn. Your soul will be refreshed.

" Had I devoted myself to birds,
their lives and plumage, I might have produced
something worth doing. "
John Ruskin

" If you have a garden and a library,
you have everything you need. "
Cicero

1. A Life of Their Own

Robins & Trilliums

I look forward each year to the spring with new life sprouting forth everywhere, the lacy fragile light green leaves appearing on the trees and the pretty pastel flowers popping up. It's always a game between Gary and me to see who can be the first to spot a robin. At the first hint of spring we should just go and check out the ground around our majestic spruce trees with their low hanging thick branches along our driveway. Upon their return from the southern states or Mexico, these cheerful songbirds with their brick red breasts head for this area where they like to build their nests and are protected. It is always unfathomable to me how these small creatures can fly that distance. Do they rent out nests from other birds along the way for a few nights like the cowbirds (more about them in another chapter)? The females, duller in color than the males, are the home builders who will soon fill their nests with 3-5 blue eggs. The robins never land on our seed station for free food. Unlike many of their bird friends they spend a lot of time hopping along the ground in search of worms. They will cock their head to one side to listen for their prey, grab it and quickly gobble it down or carry it back to their homes for their young. To me they seem to live very independently.

Our eldest daughter, Sara, has been independent from day one which can be a good thing. She takes initiative and is very capable of solving problems that others would not want to tackle. As soon as she learned to walk her greatest goal was to climb up on a wooden rocker. After a few days of practice she made it. We took pictures of her progress ending with her sitting in the chair with a huge grin on her face. Today, Sara is married to Chris and they have given us three delightful granddaughters – Cassidy, Kaiya and Carleigh. Sara is a fitness professional who leads hundreds of participants in group exercise classes each week. She is determined to motivate others towards better life, both spiritually and physically. She has written a book called From the Couch to the Stage (www.tothestage.info) – a very worthwhile read.

Conversely, several years ago a mutual friend who is very talented artistically was heavily involved in our local church. She was overcome by her independent thinking and always asking more and more questions. As a result she and her family left the church and unfortunately she and her husband of several years were divorced. She moved away to a new community close to her parents, started a new life on her own with her children and embarked on a different career path. One of my many gifts I cherish is a wooden tray hanging in our kitchen. It was hand painted by this woman. It is a picture of a robin in the spring time pulling up a worm with the Bible verse below. She also drew a couple of white trilliums as part of the background - another favorite springtime flower from the lily family which turns pink with age. Actually the trillium with its three large petals and yellow stamens has been the emblem of our province of Ontario since 1937. We are not supposed to pick them in our conservation areas; just enjoy looking at their abundance in a deciduous forest where their seeds are spread by ants.

Whenever I glance at this tray it reminds me to pray for this person whose life continues to be a struggle. My daughter periodically remains in touch and probably one day when I have passed along to meet my artistic Creator the tray will hang in her kitchen. The choices our friend has made, sadly, are not building up an important heritage for her children. It is discouraging to hear about her journey and the difficult repercussions she is facing. I often pray for God's intervention so that she may experience a true satisfying spring in her life with good independence like the robins.

But from everlasting to everlasting the Lord's love is
with those who fear him, and his righteousness
with their children's children.
Psalm 103:17

● ● ● ● ● ● ● ●
A Musing

3:37 a.m.! Really? As yet I haven't figured out which bird call, tweet, chirp or squawk belongs to which bird but possibly the robin is this extremely early riser in the spruce trees near our house. Does he want a front row seat for sunrise viewing? Eventually he does get a rise out of a friend in the next tree. I, on the other hand, am not a morning person but when I do get up a little earlier I get lots more accomplished. And then there is the part about the cheeriness. I know it would be very beneficial to all if I were to work on that attitude following my feathered friend's example.

Because of the Lord's great love we are not consumed, for his compassions never fail. They are new every morning; great is your faithfulness.
Lamentations 3:22-23.

2. Memorable Logos

Red-Winged Blackbirds & Lavatera

Male red-winged blackbirds proudly sport a Nike swoosh or logo in the center of their black wings that are colored red and yellow. When they take to flight the red becomes more predominant against their overall black glossy body. I was surprised to learn that the female is just a nondescript dark brown which makes them difficult to spot. How boring in comparison but good for camouflaging! These migratory songbirds arrive in our backyard in early spring from their winter habitat in Mexico or the southern states. They enjoy nesting near our village pond and river in the grasses or reeds. The female takes charge of all the home construction and will have babies about three times in a season in a new nursery every time. I have noticed that they can be very patient in the nearby bushes while they wait their turn on the platform of our feeder. We love to watch them smoothly soar from afar onto our seed platform. No wonder the Wright brothers long ago desperately wanted to fly like the birds. They make it look so easy.

Several years ago I discovered a tall plant with pretty pink or white flowers that I really grew to appreciate called Lavatera. It was one flower from a container of mixed flower seeds that I had thrown on the ground around our well. It bloomed from the end of July until frost. The only work it needed was some tying with string when it became quite tall and spread out. When the flower pods turned from green to black I cut them off the stems. I then took out the dried seeds which I stored in a paper envelope over winter. Every mid-May when the ground is still cold I have planted these seeds in my own garden or put them in small packets to give away as a gift, sometimes for Mother's Day in our church. I even found a business card company called VistaPrint that provided a template with a picture of a similar flower. I immediately ordered business cards and sticky notes that were very inexpensive. And so this flower has become my logo or signature flower since I have come to love so much of God's design in my garden through the years.

Christians living in the first three centuries became known for their use of a fish symbol. The Greek word, Ichthus means fish. The symbol was drawn with two intersecting arcs to resemble a fish and the accompanying letters stood for Jesus Christ, God's Son, Savior. The theme of fish is very prevalent throughout the Gospels. Some of Jesus' disciples were fishermen. The story of Jesus feeding 5000 with a little boy's bread and two fish is a favorite along with the one about the disciples fishing all night and catching nothing. Strangely enough Jesus said to cast their net on the other side of the boat and they hauled in 153! According to tradition the fish logo would identify meeting places for Christians. If two people met each would draw an arc on the road to form the symbol and thus ensure they were both Christians.

Identity is important when describing certain birds, flowers or people. Jesus emphasized that Christians will be identified for their love shown to each other. To be a better follower of Christ I must remember to ask myself when visitors come through the door of our village home, do they see that love within my home for them or do they see the annoyance of another interruption in my day's schedule? Is my home too cluttered or chaotic so that it is not a comfortable experience for them? As spouses, parents, church members too often we don't wear our Christianity very well. We must constantly tell ourselves to be proud of our faith we strongly uphold no matter the circumstances to cause it to stand out like the red-wing blackbirds' "swoosh."

By this all men will know that you are my disciples if
you love one another.
John 13:35

● ● ● ● ● ● ● ●

A Musing

Here's another question about that pre-dawn riser I mentioned previously. Is he acting as the leader to rally his choir for a great songfest? It seems that he starts and all the others join in later. Our churches need good leadership to motivate, encourage and inspire so that our members can move forward in positive harmony to accomplish great things for God's Kingdom.

Those who accepted his message {the apostle Peter}
were baptized, and about three thousand
were added to their number that day.
Acts 2:41

Lavatera

3. All Dressed Up

Cardinals & Flame Bushes

The cardinal, in my opinion, is one of the best dressed birds that God created for us to watch and enjoy. He colored the male in bright red but then for contrast gave him a black face like a bandit or raccoon. His crest (or topknot) looks like he is wearing a Mohawk hairdo. Did you know that these accomplished songsters were named after the red robes worn by Roman Catholic cardinals? Or maybe it was the other way around – the early church leaders at the beginning of their careers admired the look of these birds! The cardinals inhabit our community year round and regularly partake from our seed station in winter - most often as couples. The female is not as aggressive as the male can be. She is buff-brown, tinged with red on her crest, wings and tail. There is no better picture than a cardinal sitting on an evergreen bush after fluffy white snow has fallen – a favorite scene on many a Christmas card. However, they are stylish no matter the season.

If I were creating a preschooler's matching game of colors I would match the cardinal with the flame or burning bushes in my backyard. The leaves of this member of the euonymus family are green until the autumn when they turn a brilliant red, almost flower-like. I delight in seeing a long hedge on someone's property or a large single shrub in a park. This bush is named after the event in Exodus 3 of the Old Testament in the Bible when God caught Moses' attention through a bush on fire that did not burn up. God wanted Moses to go to the Egyptian Pharaoh regarding the oppression of his Israelite people to let them leave his country. He promised to be with Moses in this task even though he had lots of excuses.

Our second daughter, Rebekah, lives with her husband Jerome and their hockey/lacrosse loving son, Evan and ballet/jazz dance enthusiast daughter, Faith in Kelowna, BC. Bec has become quite an accomplished artist in that community. She has learned much from God's painting techniques such as the interest displayed from deliberately using contrasting colors. Rebekah was always our quiet, sensitive child while growing up in our home. One of her teachers even allowed her to stand on her desk and yell out, "I am Rebekah Carter!" She never did take him up on this exercise but the contrast in her personality today is quite interesting. With her creativity in her art she knows what she is after and has matured into a confident woman because of God's work in her life.

God catches my attention by watching the cardinals out my kitchen window to remind me that He is always with me and that my sins are forgiven. Unfortunately my flame bushes remain as dwarfs even after several years and are not very inspiring. They are supposed to be quite hardy and can grow to approximately eight feet tall. Apparently they are in too much shade so this spring one of my first garden projects will be to move them to the front yard. I am forever learning the rules of nature no matter how old I get. These rules must be followed to obtain the best gardening results. Hopefully in the years to come these ornamental bushes will catch the attention of the numerous passersby in our village. I pray that they may also rejoice in God's artistic touch all around us which will help them realize that a loving God can be with them too if only they obey His rules.

> *"Come now, let us reason together", says the Lord.*
> *"Though your sins are like scarlet, they shall be as*
> *white as snow; though they are red as crimson,*
> *they shall be like wool."*
> ***Isaiah 1:18***

A Musing

It is interesting to observe from our kitchen window how many different kinds of birds come to our seed station as couples. Many mate for life. We often saw a Mr. & Mrs. Cardinal giving each other a quick affectionate kiss with their beaks or more likely the male was handing off seeds to his wife or girlfriend. Many times she waited for him in the evergreens nearby. Was she a "kept" woman? It was very sad the day a stray black cat, we believe, snagged him for dinner. Sometimes a pair of sparrows will fly off together at the exact same time zigzagging in whatever direction to the trees beyond. They could rival any professional synchronized team of swimmers or Canada's Snowbirds performing at the airshow every August at our Canadian National Exhibition in Toronto. God's intention is marriage for life so it is important that when we see a couple that doesn't seem to be a good match we need to speak up before it is too late and they in turn must heed wise warnings before they marry. Marriage is also the support of each other's aspirations and dreams and following God's will or call on their lives together. This is not a time for "doing your own thing." It takes a lot of discussion to make it work. No withdrawal allowed!

The Lord God said, "It is not good for the man to be
alone. I will make a suitable helper for him."
Genesis 2:18

4. A Strident Sound

Blue Jays & Hydrangea

Even though rather harsh sounding, another beautiful year round bird that has been painted by God's hand is the noisy blue jay. It is predominately blue with a white breast and a black collar around its neck. There are contrasting blue dots on the tail. Male and female look identical. There's lots of great color when cardinals, blue jays and red-winged blackbirds land on our seed station at the same time. The jays look like they are walking on bouncy rubbery stilts when they start bobbing up and down while yakking away. Both husband and wife contribute in the construction of their home that will eventually house blueish or light brown eggs with brown spots. They can live up to 15 years old and have great memories particularly when they return to their caches where they have hidden extra seed for the lean times. It is interesting that our Toronto baseball team chose the name Blue Jays through a contest when they established themselves in 1977. Blue has been Toronto's traditional sporting color since 1873.

Squirrels love our free food as well but when they take up too much time I've seen a jay try to dive bomb them off the board. They sit on the roof of our well and yell shrilly at the squirrel. This all adds to the drama effect. The squirrel being in the line of fire may or may not be convinced to leave. Other birds appreciate their strident sound as it becomes an alarm system when predators like our neighbor's gray cats suddenly sneak up. Hawks and owls target the jays as they fly slower than other birds.

A perennial plant that also puts on a good show is the hydrangea that is very easy to take care of particularly when you decide to divide it and move the second portion to another location. Mine are white but they do come in other colors such as blue and pink. Their large round flower heads like pompoms cause heads to turn when placed in an ornamental flower arrangement. They bloom pretty much all summer and then the flowers turn to beige. I don't usually deadhead (cut the dead ones away) the flowers as they provide some interest in the garden over the long winter months. One of the many meanings of the word hydrangea is a sincere heart.

In I Samuel 16 in the Old Testament we read about how David, a mere shepherd boy was chosen and annointed to be the future king of the Israelite nation. It was all because of his heart. Unfortunately we as women have too often gained the reputation of reacting to our family members with strident voices, just like the jays. And the more agitated we become the sounds from our mouths become even shriller. That is not pleasant. We can spend a lot of time beautifying our appearance but if the inner heart is not sincere then bitterness, strife and envy will eventually show up in our personality in one form or another. That also is not appealing. We need to be ourselves, not a copy of someone else and show the inner beauty we own. Peter exhorts wives (I Peter 3:4) to have an "unfading beauty of a gentle and quiet spirit which is of great worth in God's sight."

> *But the Lord said to Samuel, "Do not consider his*
> *appearance or his height, for I have rejected him.*
> *The Lord does not look at the things man looks at.*
> *Man looks at the outward appearance*
> *but the Lord looks at the heart."*
> **I Samuel 16:7**

A Musing

What woman doesn't love receiving a beautiful bouquet of flowers for a special day that honors her! The choice is endless as to what can make up that bouquet with the added greenery. When the flowers are displayed in a vase as a center piece on a kitchen table or a dining-room buffet our eyes are immediately drawn to them. A cheery atmosphere is created. In our gardens hummingbirds, bees and butterflies are particularly attracted to flowers for the food they supply. God is excellent in how He shows off His artistry and provision.

As members of God's family in our churches we can show off our love, compassion and care to each other and to any outsider that pops in for a visit. If we are attractive as individuals, along with facilities that permeate a cheerful atmosphere, those visitors will feel that they are accepted no matter who they are and will want to come back for more. I must strive to be attractive like the flowers in my garden to catch the attention of both my church friends and newcomers alike.

> *... show... that in every way they will make the teaching about God our Savior attractive. For the grace of God that brings salvation has appeared to all men. It teaches us to say "no" to ungodliness and worldly passions, and to live self-controlled, upright and godly lives in this present age.*
> **Titus 2:10-12**

5. How Nervy Is That!

Cowbirds & Creeping Charlie

You ask, "So what's up with that bird?" I presented the same question to our neighbor, Sarah, that first spring we lived in our 19th century village home. We had seen brown-headed birds with glossy black bodies for the first time. She called them cowbirds that migrate as far south as Mexico each year. I couldn't believe it when she said these birds creep into other birds' nests to lay their white speckled eggs. The foster parents, usually smaller than the cowbirds, will either rear the offspring as their own or eject the unwanted egg; for example robins don't like these intruders. I subsequently have learned that the female cowbird can lay up to 40 eggs in one season. I guess they do feel the need to spread the wealth around, often to the neglect of the other birds in the nest. The cowbird babies chirp louder for food or push their smaller non-siblings out. It has been said that they are so named because they followed roving herds of bison on the grassy plains and had no time to stop to nest.

When we purchased our home there wasn't much in the backyard except for a few patches of a weed called creeping charlie (or ground ivy) here and there amidst the grass. Three or four years later charlie had taken over our whole backyard because it thrives in moist riverbed soil. No weed killer from Home Depot or the local lawn care service could banish him. This weed is like a vine that travels on the surface of the ground under the grass or propagates itself through its seeds. It does have attractive leaves and pretty tiny lavender flowers in the spring that make it easier to see for weeding. It is a favorite green in a salad with its peppermint taste in many countries around the world and has been used for medicinal purposes in Europe. Again my next-door answer lady suggested I try sprinkling a mixture of Borax and water (8 oz. of

Borax dissolved in 2 gallons of hot water to cover 1000 square feet) on this unwanted creeper which solution she had learned from the Internet. After applying the mixture the green leaves started turning brown and the lawn became bare as there wasn't much grass left. In a few weeks I did some extra seeding and hand weeding. Amazingly enough my lawn now looks great as I have controlled charlie even though he has not disappeared completely. How cool is that!

Sin is a creeper and sometimes puts on a good appearance. I wish I could eliminate it like getting rid of an annoying weed but that will not happen during life on this earth. It will always creep back. In the third chapter of Genesis we learn about Satan portrayed as a serpent that was cursed by God and required to stealthily crawl on his belly. When he raises his ugly head of selfishness, fear, apathy, lack of faith, a critical spirit, laziness etc. in my life instantaneously or over time, I must remember to look to Christ. Through His death, burial and resurrection, He has forgiven me such merciless sins and so many more for now and eternity. It is deeply sad to watch an addict's life gradually become totally controlled by the drugs or food they crave and the lies they tell to get those waste-producing dependencies. Thankfully, I freely accepted God's offer of adoption as a child of eight and became one of His legitimate daughters. I do not need to cheat like the cowbirds in our backyard who try to get more than their fair share at our seed station. Nor will God ever eject me out of His nest.

> *So the Lord God said to the serpent, "Because you*
> *have done this, cursed are you above all the livestock*
> *and all the wild animals! You will crawl on your belly*
> *and you will eat dust all the days of your life..."*
> **Genesis 3:14**

A Musing

If perchance Gary misses one day putting seed out for the birds they keep landing on the feeder in search of food. They are creatures of habit. One morning a squirrel climbed up on the platform and when he discovered no food he stared at Gary through the window as if to demand, "Quit eating your breakfast and bring me mine!" Every spring our perennial flowers, even though they look dead in winter, sprout forth anew to bloom for our delight. God created man also as a creature of habit. I can't believe how many church attenders like to sit in the same pew/chair every single Sunday (me included)! Forming good habits and getting rid of bad habits is the way to live.

Every day they continued to meet together in the temple courts. They broke bread in their homes and ate together with glad and sincere hearts, praising God and enjoying the favor of all the people.
Acts 2:46-47

6. Are Doves Really Peaceful?

Doves & Lilies

So does the plaintive cooing of mourning doves make you feel relaxed and contented or does it become annoying to you after time? These buff colored birds with black spots on their wings, pink feet and legs and long tails would visit our seed station any time of the year if there were seed for them. They remind me of a large cargo plane with their fat bellies when they land on the board to fuel up. Often one will just sit a spell to rest. We have seen up to 12 birds feeding at once but many times we have noticed one guy who wants to be king and will peck the others until he has the station all to himself. Often he will sit on the pile of seed. Someone needs to notify this irritable leader that his white cousin has been a symbol of peace in our Christian faith since Noah's day (Genesis 8:11). Noah sent out a dove from his huge boat to find land after the flood rains stopped. On its second journey it returned with an olive leaf in its beak. The female of our dove version looks similar to the male and will lay two white eggs up to six times in a season. They are very devoted as parents. They are strong fliers, often traveling about 88 kilometers an hour. Sadly too often, we have found a pile of feathers on the lawn after a wandering cat has snatched one up for his dinner.

Tiger lilies (or ditch lilies) are a remembrance of lazy, warm summer days when our family headed out on vacation. Wherever you travel in Ontario these tall spotted orange flowers swaying in the breeze grow prolifically along the roadsides in moist soil to brighten up your journey. White lilies with their strong perfume are often called the "white-robed apostles of hope" and add to the celebration of the resurrection of Jesus Christ every spring. Too much of their perfume, however, can give me a headache. Lilies are the earliest recorded flower in history which grow from bulbs or tuberous roots. These perennial plants have lovely trumpet-shaped flowers and come in many colors and species. They are easy to grow and no problem to dig out a clump to move to another location; except they do tend to take over an area in your garden if you aren't watching.

Our family growing up looked forward to whatever kind of vacation every year that was scheduled, often heading to a favorite cottage near Arnstein, ON on a little lake. Good memories were built around this cottage without electricity, only propane. I have lots of picture albums and now computer files to prove it. The importance of this tradition has been passed along to our children and their children. What a great stress buster and worry defuser in a society that seems to be running faster and faster to catch up. Our souls crave for a time of peace. A few of my favorite verses that I memorized growing up are found in Matthew 11:28-30, "Come to me, all you who are weary and burdened, and I will give you rest. Take my yoke upon you and learn from me, for I am gentle and humble in heart and you will find rest for your souls. For my yoke is easy and my burden is light."

Consider how the lilies grow. They do not labor
or spin. Yet I tell you, not even Solomon in all his
splendor was dressed like one of these. If that is
how God clothes the grass of the field, which is here
today, and tomorrow is thrown in the fire, how much
more will he clothe you, O you of little faith?
Luke 12:27-28

A Musing

Bigger and better and new and improved always catches our attention. Horticulturalists strive for producing hardier plants with more variety in colorful flowers. Have you ever heard about a lily tree that blooms mid-summer every year? I have one in my garden that grows strong and sturdy from a bulb. About 4-5 blooms appear on the main stem.

Since it can grow up to eight feet tall it is ideal to be planted at the back of a garden.

If you study the Bible you will learn about the Israelite people in the Old Testament who were given the law of Moses to live by – 10 simple rules. Time and time again they broke these rules and fell into sin; they couldn't do it on their own, even the most faithful among them. God's better plan was to send His Son Jesus Christ to earth to live among these Israelite people for over 30 years. Some learned to love Him and many others rejected Him. As a result He was crucified on a cross. That death process satisfied God's desire to deal with everyone's sin - Israelites and non-Israelites. He rose from the dead after three days and then ascended into heaven soon after to be with God. All we have to do is believe what happened, repent over our sins, accept His forgiveness and let Him be the boss of our lives.

These were all commended for their faith, yet none
of them received what had been promised. God had
planned something better for us so that
only together with us would they be made perfect.
Hebrews 11:39-40

7. Standing Tall Like Soldiers

Grackles & Irises

The common grackle was another migratory bird that I was not familiar with before our move to Churchville. In the early spring all of a sudden six or seven of these sociable creatures just seem to appear on our seed station where they will first snag the corn pellets. About the same size as a blue jay, they have a dark glossy head with a neck that is actually quite iridescent depending on the light that reveals blue, purple, green, bronze colors. The rest of the body is brownish black. God's finishing touch is the bright yellow circle painted around their eyes. They like to be around water. Our Credit River (see Addendum A) flowing through the centre of our village does it nicely for them. Their voice is high pitched, somewhat sounding like a squeaky hinge. They like to mimic other birds. Maybe that is all part of their scheme to steal their food. Often we will see a couple of grackles perched on the top of the roof of our well in our backyard. They will be standing tall, stretching their necks and beaks to the sky as if searching for airplanes that fly overheard every few minutes. Their eyes are very piercing.

Iris, my crafty Swedish mother was a doer and a survivor who died a few years ago at the age of 95. Everyone marveled at the beautiful, colorful quilts (50 over her lifetime) she hand sewed and her lovely colorful garden which she carefully tended up until her last year with us. Many of her flowers and bushes became part of our landscape when we sold her home. One of her favorite showy flowers was her namesake, the iris which is derived from the Greek word for rainbow since it comes in so many different colors. She admired the way they stood tall like soldiers along her backyard fence in later May and June. Blue miniatures, a gift from a neighbor, bloom at the side of our yard in early spring as well. The flag of Quebec displays four stylized white fleurs-de-lis (an iris type) on blue background in each corner between a white cross. Vincent Van Gogh is famous for his iris paintings (my artist daughter would be impressed with my knowledge!). This perennial plant from the lily family thrives on well-drained soil in a sunny spot. Mine have got to be moved from one side of the yard to the other. Their bulbous roots live near the surface of the earth and should be covered with mulch or dried leaves for protection from winter freezing or heaving. I must remember to do that this fall.

Gary and I have labored together in the local church wherever we have lived throughout our marriage (46 years in 2014) and have made decisions that come from much discussion and unity. We have experienced joyful, satisfying times along with discouraging, unhappy times. When a church member is excited about getting their act together and after a few years we see him/her flourish as a mature follower of Christ, we feel extremely fulfilled. That person has developed into a strong soldier for the cross of Christ. When a church member has been disgruntled with my husband as pastor due to lack of understanding or ego getting in the way, as his wife I am very sad and hurt. However, I still must let him solve his own problems in that position all the while standing behind him in prayer. No matter the circumstances, happy or difficult, we have learned to stand tall and firm with Christ's help just like my mom and her irises. We know that our Lord considers our work has not been in vain.

> *Therefore, my dear brothers and sisters, stand firm.*
> *Let nothing move you. Always give yourselves*
> *fully to the work of the Lord, because you know*
> *that your labor in the Lord is not in vain.*
> **1 Corinthians 15:58**

A Musing

"Bloom where you are planted." was a popular quote years ago. The goal of any good gardener is to keep color happening from early spring to late fall around the yard. Perennial plants that grow up every year only last for a few weeks in a season so it can be a challenge as they cycle through and we try to maintain proper balance. God's Word is an important standard for us to follow so that we can bloom in the situation we find ourselves until it is the right time for Him to take us up to our heavenly home.

> *The grass withers and the flowers fall because the*
> *breath of the Lord blows on them. Surely the people*
> *are grass. The grass withers and the flowers fall*
> *but the word of our God stands forever.*
> ***Isaiah 40:7-8***

8. A Rosy Picture

Purple Finches & Weigela

So what color is the purple finch? Surprisingly, the male is not purple but rather rosy in color on his head, upper breast, back and rump. He sports a white belly. Every once in a while throughout the year this little flying creature with its musical warble will confidently land on our platform feeder among several birds, many twice his size. Some one has said it looks like he has been dipped in raspberry juice. The female is light brown streaked with dark brown and has a white belly and a white band on its face. How different is that from the male! In our culture it's usually the woman who likes to be dressed in bright colors. Finches love eating sunflower seeds. After its fill of food I watched one particular rosy fellow take off. He just kept flying east over our neighbor's farm field and in about ten seconds reached the trees near the pond on the other side. It seemed he was on a mission. He knew where he was going without any hesitation for he had a path he was following.

We have two rosy-colored weigela (a name I stumble over every time which should be pronounced why-jee´-lah) bushes about six feet high. They were a memorial gift from some friends after my dad died a few years ago. They are located on either side of the door of our little barn on the pathway to our backyard. They certainly add much beauty in later May and June to our garden with their prolific amount of bell-shaped flowers which attract hummingbirds and butterflies. As with many flowering shrubs the flowers should be clipped soon after they have bloomed. I get a few blooms a second time round later in the summer if I'm fortunate. When pruning weigela, I've learned to trim back about one-third of a branch a little above a shoot or a bud. Flowers will grow next year on new wood that develops this year. Old wood that is 1 ½ inches in diameter can be cut out. It was probably more by accident but where I planted them is a good spot because they are in full sun and the soil is well-drained.

Phyllis was a wonderful mother-in-law who died several years ago. Whenever she and Gary's dad came for a few days to visit when our children were young, she would dig right in to help. She would iron the clothes, clean the oven, and cook a few meals. She even taught me how to bake my first apple pie when Gary and I were newly married. She didn't give out a lot of advice but one piece she did recommend was to make friends with younger people so that you still have friends when you get older. More importantly she lived her Christian life before us all. I remember her sitting at our kitchen table after breakfast in a pink dress. She would be reading her Bible and praying. Her favorite Bible verses below were from the King James version. She confidently loved the Lord who directed her path through life over 80 years. No matter her age she was often found helping out in the nursery at the church she loved where she was a charter member. Now that was a rosy picture indeed that we dearly miss along with her constant prayers on our behalf.

Trust in the LORD with all thine heart; and lean
not unto thine own understanding. In all thy ways
acknowledge him, and he shall direct thy paths.
Proverbs 3:5-6

A Musing

We find Jesus praying in the Garden of Gethsemane in John 18 of the New Testament. Gethsemane means the "oil press" and the "Garden" was probably an olive yard. A lot of the time during the month of May I can be found in my gardens tidying them up after the winter season, trimming back bushes and trees, transplanting old flowers and planting new, mulching etc. During all those working hours I tell God how grateful I am for His hand in my life and the wonderful surroundings

He has provided. I also pray about the numerous needs in my own life, in Gary's life and direction for our future as an older couple in ministry, for our children and their children, for our church and its family members, for our friends and neighbors, for our church denomination, for our beloved country and so much more. The beautiful sky above is the limit and God will hear everyone of those prayers.

> *When he had finished praying, Jesus left with his*
> *disciples and crossed the Kidron Valley. On the*
> *other side there was an olive grove, and he and his*
> *disciples went into it. Now Judas, who betraying*
> *him, knew the place, because Jesus*
> *had often met there with his disciples.*
> ***John 18:12***

> *Then Jesus went with his disciples to a place called*
> *Gethsemane, and he said to them,*
> *"Sit here while I go over there and pray."*
> ***Matthew 26:36***

9. Be strong and Courageous!

Woodpeckers & Manitoba Maples

Woodpeckers like to hammer on wood or anything else they think is wood. They can peck at a tree up to 300 times a minute or 8-12,000 times in a day. At one of our previous homes we watched a woodpecker from our window continue to strike our neighbour's aluminum siding to look for insects but I don't think he was successful even though he tried it for several days. The black and white downy woodpeckers (males have a dab of red on the back of their necks) in Churchville also like to peck at the side of our barn. God has created this little strong creature with several body parts that help him in his task - strong muscles at the base of the beak and neck give power and help absorb the shock of the thrust; feet have sharp curved nails for clinging; tail feathers are stiff to act as a prop; the tongue extends to retrieve insects in tunnel crevices. The woodpecker even knows to close its eyes for further protection as it drills a hole in a tree for building a new nest every spring. What didn't God think of!

Manitoba maples (or box elders) grow throughout Churchville because it is a flood plain area. Even though quite large these sprawling trees are not very strong particularly in extreme wind or ice. We lose several every winter. They grow fast and die fast. I came home from work one summer's day and as I approached our driveway near the bottom of our hill was a wall of leaves - a huge branch had just fallen across the road due to a very strong rainstorm. I was glad I didn't have to travel any further. Then when I went into the kitchen I saw that another gigantic branch from the maple in the back corner was lying on the garden between our property and our neighbor's. There was not much damage to the plants but there was lots of labor in cutting up smaller branches and carting them away. Manufacturers like the soft wood for constructing boxes or fiberboard. These trees attract a docile, household nuisance called a Manitoba maple bug (black with red spots on the back) that gets into our homes through crevices or cracks. The only solution to get rid of these harmless insects is to seal up the cracks if you can find the hidden openings. Not too many people like these "trash" trees as sometimes nicknamed; except they do make a good home for the squirrels who love eating the buds in the spring and the seeds that are produced. Small yellow green flowers bloom in April.

The sixth book of the Old Testament tells the story of Joshua being commanded by God to finally lead the Israelite people from their journeys in the wilderness and cross over the Jordan River into Canaan country to the west, God's promised land for them. Several times God reminds Joshua that he needed to be strong and courageous. God was going to be with him each step of the way throughout this new adventure. My choice in life, like Joshua's, is to either be strong like the woodpecker because I am depending on my God or weak and insignificant without much direction like the Manitoba maple that breaks down when the going gets tough.

> *Have I not commanded you? Be strong and*
> *courageous. Do not be terrified;*
> *do not be discouraged, for the Lord your God*
> *will be with you wherever you go.*
> **Joshua 1:9**

A Musing

Birds are always aware of their surroundings particularly when they land on our platform for food. They keep turning their heads this way and that to make sure no enemy tries to attack. They will fly to the top of a nearby tree to get a "bird's eye view" and thus the expression. Their eyesight is their most important sense especially for flying. Birds that have eyes at the side of their head obtain a wide or landscape view while those that have eyes at the front like owls have "binocular" vision which allows them to see prey they want to hunt from a distance.

It must be dreadful to live without sight so I guess that is why one of my favorite Bible stories in the New Testament is about Jesus giving sight to the man born blind. All of chapter 9 in the Gospel of John is an interesting study. How excited the man must have been when he realized he could see all of his surroundings. He even saw the angry looks on the Pharisees' faces as they investigated this healing miracle and accused him of being one of Jesus' disciples. After they threw him out of the synagogue Jesus found him again and healed him of his spiritual blindness as well. It is sad to see how spiritually blind those who live around us are just like the Pharisees in this story. They resist hearing any information about Jesus.

> *He replied, "Whether he is a sinner or not, I don't know. One thing I know. I was blind but now I see!"*
> **John 9:25**

10. No Matter How Small

Hummingbirds & Asters

Don't blink or you will lose sight of the small male ruby-throated hummingbird that flew by our kitchen window. It was looking for nectar with its needle-like bill from the May tubular blossoms of our pink beauty bush by the porch or the weigela near the barn. They also like my purple phlox and lavender butterfly bush which bloom throughout the summer and fall. These non-sociable, very small birds, 7–9 cm (2.8–3.5 in) in length, are metallic green, white and black. Their body weight is 25-30% muscle and their wings attach to their bodies from the shoulder joint which allow the wings to rotate close to 180° so the bird can fly both forwards and backwards. They hover in front of the flowers or catch tiny insects mid-air while their wings beat 55 times per second. They spend their winters in southern Mexico, Central and South America and the West Indies which means they have to fly 500 miles across the Gulf of Mexico. This non-stop flight demands incredible endurance.

I was surprised the other day to see that my miniature aster plant that I had purchased a few years back was finally blooming purple flowers with yellow centers. The name aster comes from the ancient Greek word for star that describes the shape of the flower head. These flowers most often come in white, pink, blue, purple or violet. They make a great filler in floral arrangements. I'm not sure why as a small child I took a fancy to these pretty flowers in my mom's garden. I remember seeing them in other gardens as well and liked the dark violet ones in particular. Part of my heritage was belonging to a Swedish community of extended relatives and friends who were very close-knit. The thing to do when visiting in each other's homes was to take a tour of the garden – maybe to trade gardening tips. My Aunt Helen's garden was immaculately beautiful. I presume at that point in society there were not many mothers who worked outside of the home. They often put their creativity into their gardening skills along with the knowledge they brought from "the old country" that resulted in outside accomplishments they could be very proud of. My grandmother loved her garden.

"I'm like that too!" exclaimed Cassidy, one of our older granddaughters. She was responding to a remark her father had made about himself. I was noticing that she and her sister, Kaiya, were hanging around listening more and more to adult conversation. The main language spoken at Swedish get-togethers was Swedish and so as a child I didn't know what was being said much of the time; although I did have friends my age to play with who spoke English. Since I had never learned the language I was in the dark a fair bit of the time and I believe my faith suffered somewhat because of that indirect adult Christian influence. Today Christian parents have to contend with all the various distractions afforded to their children such as sports programs, video games, television, schooling etc. In the long run one has to figure out what is the best direction to take children no matter how small they are. Jesus said in Mark 10:14, "...Let the little children come to me, and do not hinder them, for the kingdom of God belongs to such as these." Our daughter, Sara, has written a song for our church. The first line goes, "Don't get in the way of the faith of a child..."

Teach them to your children, talking about them when you sit at home and when you walk along the road, when you lie down and when you get up.
Deuteronomy 11:19

A Musing

Through my recent ornithological (I like that word!) studies I have learned how the majority of birds (cowbirds excluded) do really take care of their children. They are great teachers. When the babies are old enough the parents will remain a short distance away from the nest to give them some space. When they get hungry and no food automatically arrives, to survive the children are forced to get out of their nest. After a few falls combined with some amount of instinct and practice they soon figure it out with continued help from their parents. During the summer months we have seen smaller birds that must be offspring of some sparrows. The other day I watched a mother songbird sparrow fluttering its wings at the young one with her and putting seed into its mouth. The little bird pecked some seed for himself from the board. Then off they flew together.

It is discouraging to hear about a new believer in Christ who does not get proper follow-up or teaching after the very important, life-changing decision they have made. Good teaching is vital for them to produce maturity and loyalty in their new found faith. The writer of Hebrews thoroughly understood that process. First of all infants require milk but then as they grow older they can move on to more solid food.

> *... by this time you ought to be teachers, you need*
> *someone to teach you the elementary truths of God's*
> *word all over again. You need milk, not solid food!*
> *Anyone who lives on milk, being still an infant, is not*
> *acquainted with the teaching about righteousness.*
> *But solid food is for the mature, who by constant use*
> *have trained themselves to distinguish*
> *good from evil.*
> ***Hebrews 5:12-14***

11. Get Your Ducks in a Row

Ducks & Tulips

Everyone loves strolling or biking or driving to the bridge over our Credit River. It is only a two minute walk from our home. Avid fishermen enjoy fishing along the banks. Unfortunately the beavers chomped down the small trees that were planted nearby a couple of years ago. The bridge is a great place for conversations with neighbors along with viewing ducks and geese swimming in the rapid water below. Springtime is baby time. It's fun watching innocent downy creatures trail after their mother on the land or water and thus we get one origin of the idiom "get your ducks in a row." Recently on the news we watched with bated breath a mother duck with her ducklings unexpectedly crossing a very busy eight lane highway. They were inches from getting smashed by speeding cars. They did make it to the other side but I sure don't know what was on that mother's mind. What was so good about the other side? This was not the best parenting which is unusual for these birds who do take really good care of their offspring.

Tulips are another springtime perennial flower I enjoy. I have planted pastel purple and pink ones in the garden at the front of our home. Just as they start popping out of the ground I place half a dryer sheet near them covered with some stones or mud so it doesn't blow away in the wind. My tulip heads don't get chomped off by the squirrels who stay away from the smell of the sheets. Also they tend to go after the younger plants that have not bloomed year after year. I cut the stocks halfway down after blooming so the nutrition heads for the roots. The rest of the foliage will eventually dry up and die. I must remember not to plant something else in the same spot or I won't be happy with myself the next spring. Tulip bulbs are planted in the fall. Our nation's capital of Ottawa prides itself in its Canadian Tulip Festival every May – the largest in the world displaying over one million flowers. The tulip is symbolic in Canada's role in freeing the Dutch during World War II, particularly for providing a safe place for the Dutch Royal family. In 1945 the Netherlands sent over 100,000 bulbs to thank us for taking care of Princess Julilana and her daughters for three years. 10,000 more have been sent each year thereafter. Rows and rows of tulips of the same color in gardens add beauty throughout the city.

Our son, Rob and his family recently traveled to California to see the whales and to Arizona to see the Grand Canyon. The three oldest girls know exactly what is expected of them when they walk through an airport. Each one wears a knapsack on their back and carries a car seat to use in the van when they get to their destination. Jess carries the baby and both parents guide them around other travelers with baggage carts through the long hallways to embark on their next plane. Coming from Moosonee it is a long haul for them all. Growing up at home I would always walk by an ornate wooden plaque that was hung in my parents' hallway. It was inscribed "Jesus always cares – He careth for you." (King James Version). Those words took me through many a year back then and the plaque is now hanging in my own hallway. So what benefit is there to worry when Jesus has made this promise to care for us like a father? It only adds more gray hairs to the ones I already have. I need to get my ducks in a row better than I do. He expects that of me.

Cast all your anxiety on him
because he cares for you.
I Peter 5:7

A Musing

Water, along with good sunlight, is vital to plant life. I generally don't mind the labor involved in maintaining a garden. I can cope with dirt getting under my finger nails. But I have the hardest time with making sure the soil in my gardens or flower boxes doesn't dry out. Pulling out the hose or watering can is a chore. A hydrange plant grows behind the back of our barn out of reach of my hose. When I don't give it specific attention the leaves quickly shrivel up as do my impatiens blooms along the porch. Mulching (such as grass clippings, shredded bark, wood chips, shredded newspaper or mini bark nuggets which I like best) helps to enrich the soil and decreases moisture evaporation. But when God sends a gentle, all day rain I am most grateful.

Water is also vital to human life to promote proper health and energy. Dehydration can cause damage in the body. I notice that when I haven't had enough water my legs will cramp while I am laying in bed at night. The Samaritan woman knew the importance of water but when she met Jesus at the well she learned about the living water He provides that is far superior.

> *... Everyone who drinks this water will be thirsty*
> *again, but whoever drinks the water I give him will*
> *never thirst. Indeed, the water I give him*
> *will become in him a spring of water*
> *welling up to eternal life.*
> ***John 4:13-14***

12. Uniqueness is A Good Thing!

Black-Capped Chickadees & Bleeding Hearts

I like the curious black-capped chickadees that frequent our seed station year round. Their black toupees, black beards and white underpants cause them to be very striking in appearance. Their nests can often be found in a hole in a rotten tree. They tend to be rather nervous when they sit on the platform and continually peer around for predators. These cute creatures of God are so very different than all the other birds. The ones living in our village don't fly in as a family like the sparrows to the feeder but will arrive one at a time. They are named after the song they sing – chick-a-dee-dee-dee. They will always take just one seed and fly away again to a nearby bush. They use up a lot of energy with this constant feeding pattern. Maybe they believe that exercise should be a key component in their lives. Our fitness instructor daughter would whole-heartedly agree with them. They also like to hang upside down from a branch in search of eggs or larvae from insects. I am told that they are easily tamed and will even learn to feed from one's hand. That would be a new challenge to take on.

Bleeding heart flowers are also very different from any other flowers. If you look closely at them their symmetry in design is amazing. I can't be convinced that a God of order isn't responsible. These unique perennial plants appear each May in the shady part of my garden. The little delicate pink and white heart-shaped flowers look like they are hanging on a clothesline. At the bottom of each heart it seems as if there is a drop of blood dangling. They have become a symbol of undying love through the centuries. Since their foliage tends to dry out and die after they have bloomed I have found it advantageous to surround them with other plants like hostas that will fill in the area throughout the rest of the summer and fall.

Jesus tells a parable or story about a farmer sowing seed in Matthew 13 which is repeated in Mark 4 and Luke 8. He described four different kinds of soil where the seeds landed. Some seed fell along a path where birds swiped them up to devour them; some fell on rocky ground with no soil so could not take root; some fell among thorns which choked them out of their existence; and other seed fell on good soil where the plants flourished. Jesus subsequently interprets the seed as being the good message He brought to mankind. Some don't understand it; some immediately receive it but through hard times forget about it quickly; some can't get past their daily worries or wealth concerns. Fortunately others do understand and become very fruitful in their lives. God has made each one of us very different as individuals with our own thinking capacity and choice of will for decision making. We don't have to copy another person's appearance, lifestyle, or personality. We just have to be ourselves. I find that hard to do as a pastor's wife because I always want to please everyone. Be beautiful in your own way along with choosing Him.

Then he told them many things in parables, saying:
"A farmer went out to sow his seed. As he was
scattering the seed, some fell along the path, and the
birds came and ate it up. Some fell on rocky places,
where it did not have much soil. It sprang up quickly,
because the soil was shallow. But when the sun came
up, the plants were scorched, and they withered
because they had no root. Other seed fell among
thorns, which grew up and choked the plants.
Still other seed fell on good soil,
where it produced a crop..."
Matthew 13: 4-7

A Musing

Whenever I am out gardening I hear a bird call that to me sounds like a male or female singing, "Greener! Greener!" I haven't as yet discovered which bird it is but as I look around me our home is definitely surrounded in green. We are not lacking in vegetation so why this constant message? Enough already. I get it. I can say for one thing about this feathered creature, he certainly is persistent. However he is really just going about his business from one day to the next saying the same thing over and over. He is a great example to us as we daily carry out Christ's mandate in our lives. We have a very compelling, understandable message that does need to be spread to all those who are willing to hear.

He said to them, "Go into all the world
and preach the good news to all creation.
Whoever believes and is baptized will be saved,
but whoever does not believe will be condemned."
Mark 16:15-16

13. Wanted or Not

Crows & Snow-On-the-Mountain

One summer afternoon our neighbor Ross decided he didn't want to listen any longer to the noisy flock of cawing crows high up in the trees on his property. He started banging on some metal equipment for several minutes which surprisingly scared them away. These pidgeon-sized stocky black birds with fan-shaped tails are often seen scavenging dead carrion along our highways or country roads. Their diet is diverse but they have never landed on our feeder to our knowledge. The American crow is considered to be among the world's most intelligent animals, sometimes imitating the human voice or sounds of other animals or birds. Their age span can be up to 20 years. Their offspring will hang around for a couple of years to help with the rearing of newer babies. Since they are highly sociable they will be seen in a group rather than alone. Even though a strong bird they are susceptible to the West Nile virus. This is an indication that the disease may be in the area when a dead bird is discovered.

Snow-on-the-mountain (or Bishop's Weed) is a very pretty plant with green leaves edged in ivory. Its flowers are white clusters. I bought a small container for $5 at a local nursery and innocently planted this invasive perennial along the side of our little barn. I have been kicking myself ever since. Wow, does it ever spread and it is really hard to eliminate for the white flowers become seeds. I no longer want it in my garden. I must dig out the whole root system and then cover the area with black tarp or plastic so it doesn't come back.

Our eldest son, Robin, was very much wanted. When he was born my mother asked if we were sure we got a boy after two girls. Somewhere along the way Gary nicknamed him "Crow." Apparently the idea of nicknames has recently become a positive fatherhood tip to follow for it gives a child a feeling of safety and self-esteem in the home as the child gets older. Who would have thought?

When growing up in our home Rob was always very determined to the point of becoming annoying when he had something on his mind such as buying a skate board, unicycle or a new guitar. And when the certain toy or instrument was finally purchased he would practice day and night. His wife, Jessica, says he is like a dog on a bone. He fell in love with music as an early teen when Gary taught him to play a few chords on his old guitar. He went on to master trumpet and drums in high school as well. Because of his determination and persistent attitude he has become a true "bushwhacker" while living in Moosonee, ON (located at the tip of the James Bay) with its long, cold winters. He and Jess are raising four pretty, active daughters – Sydney, Ava & Jade (twins) and Isabella. Rob is on the elders' board at their church which is trying to reach out to the surrounding needy Cree community. He periodically travels overseas for short term musical ministry to such restrictive countries as Turkey, Kyrgystan, Kazakhstan, Albania and more. This can get rather risky at times because of the political atmosphere in the particular country. As parents we are very grateful that God has made good use of Rob's strong personality traits wherever possible to accomplish great things for His Kingdom.

I can do everything through him
who gives me strength.
Philippians 4:13

A Musing

Poverty among our backyard birds never seems to be an issue as it is with mankind. Our food supply does help their cause but generally they all seem very healthy. It just makes it easier for them particularly during long cold winter months with lots of snow covering the ground.

God is our great faithful provider. Gary and I have proved Him to be true time and time again during any adverse circumstances we are hit with. We never know what He will send around the next corner to keep us going. Because we try to live righteously before Him, we "thrive like a green leaf" as Proverbs 11:28 reminds us.

And to all the beasts of the air and all the creatures
that move on the ground – everything that has breath
of life in it – I give every green plant for food.
And it was so.
Genesis 1:30

14. Families Stay Together

Sparrows & Impatiens

The little active house sparrow is the most widely distributed bird throughout the world. At several times these birds were introduced to North America. 50 pairs from England were brought to Brooklyn, NY in 1852 to adopt a new country. The rest is history with the resulting abundance on this continent. It really is true that "birds of a feather flock together." Sometimes we see one lonely guy feasting on our seeds. Soon he is joined by twelve more of his relatives. Then in a few seconds they all leave at the spur of the moment flying in the same direction. Which one yelled, "Flee!"? At some point you must have seen them all lined up on a telephone line on a country road. They stick closely to their family but still are very sociable and easy going for they will feed alongside many other different species. The females are pale brown and grey while the males have brighter black, brown and white markings. They prefer to nest in tree holes, eaves or house crevices and will often take over an unused nest. These birds are generally monogamous mating for life. We also have song and chipping sparrows in our village. Us old timers remember delighting in hearing Mahalia Jackson's deep-voiced rendering of the Gospel hymn, His Eye is on the Sparrow.

Impatiens flowers (colored in pink, white, red, or purple) have become one of the most predominant annual bedding plants in North America. This flower family thrives in rich, moist soil in the shade and will flourish up to about a foot high. They are great for my flower boxes on the railing of our front porch. I add some white stones after planting so the squirrels don't dig them out of the boxes. My favorite color is salmon/pink because of the contrast to the white railing. They bloom from the end of May until frost kills them in the fall. They are so easy to live with requiring only water every few days – no clipping or deadheading. By the way, our five-year old granddaughter, Carleigh, refers to deadheading as picking off the old "rusty" blooms.

Lee, our South Korean youngest son always wanted a family. It was a family decision to choose and adopt him when he was almost six in 1986. We wanted to be more involved than just sending money overseas. Lee had been abandoned on a doorstep as a baby. Upon his discovery he was placed in a Christian orphanage. Our case study was matched with his. From the first day he became part of our Carter clan. With his winsome smile and social butterfly behavior Lee made it to adulthood. God has had his eye on this light brown "sparrow" for he married his Christian friend, Melissa. They have a three-year old son that looks just like his father as a baby. The orphanage staff had sent us his picture. They were thrilled to have Lee and his family return to visit in 2011. Baby Sophia was born in 2013.

Horticulturalists will graft a branch of a tree or plant into the trunk or stem of a different kind. The branch is taped at the join and covered with graft wax to hold it in place until it grows as part of the original. Many of the apples we purchase today are grown on dwarfed apple trees. Our easy-going son from Korea was grafted into our family and permanently belongs to Gary and me, his parents and to God. Often people will be surprised he is our son but we truly have forgotten about the difference in looks since the day he stepped off the airplane in New York City. Within the year he became officially adopted as a Canadian citizen at age six.

Religion that God our Father accepts as pure
and faultless is this:
to look after orphans and widows ...
James 1:27

A Musing

Every once in a while a bird will fly into our kitchen window. Gary and I will both wince when that happens. I am sure that hurts. Somehow they are able to pick themselves up and fly away in the opposite direction. I have hung a sun catcher in the window but it doesn't seem to deter them much. I hope it's not the same bird each time! In like manner, it is really hard to stand by and watch your children, no matter the age, all of a sudden fly into a "kitchen window." As parents we look on, try to warn them of danger, pray for God's protection on their lives and then sadly pick up their pieces as much as we can. Did you sing the song below as a child in Sunday School? The lyrics and music were composed by Maria and Solomon Straub in 1874.

God sees the little sparrow fall,
It meets His tender view;
If God so loves the little birds,
I know He loves me, too.
Refrain:
He loves me, too, He loves me, too,
I know He loves me, too;
Because He loves the little things,
I know He loves me, too.
He paints the lily of the field,
Perfumes each lily bell;
If He so loves the little flow'rs,
I know He loves me well.
God made the little birds and flow'rs,
And all things large and small;
He'll not forget his little ones,
I know He loves them all.

Are not two sparrows sold for a penny?
Yet not one of them will fall to the ground
apart from the will of your Father.
Matthew 10:29

15. Beware of the Danger!

Hawks & Thorns

The hawk is one of the worst enemies of smaller birds such as the blue jays, often snatching them mid-air with their powerful talons. Their eyesight is incredible and thus the term "hawk-eyed." Their vision is 20/2 instead of our 20/20 so that they can view an object as if it were only two feet away instead of 20 feet as humans do. They love to soar over the pond that is beyond our neighbor's property. When our kids were young we enjoyed driving down to Port Stanley from St. Thomas where we lived at the time to watch the hawks on a beautiful autumn day. They would be circling above the cliffs along Lake Erie to catch an updraft of wind to send them on their migration journey south. The female is larger than the male and their wing span can vary from 42 to 56 inches (107 to 141 cm). We have 15 different species of hawks in Ontario.

It was probably a beige and white red-tailed hawk that I spied from my kitchen window one morning. He was sitting on the fence just behind the tall cedars about ten feet from our seed station. He, in turn, was spying on our bird and squirrel visitors. Was he the one that all of a sudden swooped down from the sky towards the feeder while we were eating lunch a few days later? He didn't catch any prey for his dramatic efforts but the grey squirrel immediately jumped from the feeder over to our porch stairs. This terrified animal stayed there for about five minutes trying to calm his poor beating heart. Beware of the hawks!

Thorns or thistles are another unwelcome enemy in my garden or lawn. They can be dangerous when our small grandchildren run about on the soft grass. A sudden sharp pain by a thorn invading the bottom of a tender bare foot deserves every traumatic fallen tear. Thistles will choke out other plants I want in an area if I'm not diligent in weeding them. And because of the thorns which have poked my fingers too many times, I'm not really partial to roses. The Canada thistle is very common and actually has a pretty purple flower that blooms throughout the summer. Ontario's ban on the cosmetic use of pesticides has made our task of getting rid of these weeds a lot harder. My trusty spade-like shovel works very well for me during spring, summer and fall particularly if it is well sharpened. Beware of the thistles and thorns!

Thunk! "What on earth was that noise?" I wondered as I sat relaxing and reading one evening in our upstairs bedroom. After quite a few seconds I finally moved myself to go and investigate. I opened our front door and saw the red tail lights of a car that someone was trying to hurriedly turn around in our driveway. All of a sudden the car scooted onto the street and headed away up the hill out of sight. Apparently in very short order the driver had sped down our notoriously steep hill, lost control, spun out into our driveway, and hit the corner of our white porch plus the rear end of our car. We have no idea the damage on his car but we incurred $4000 in expenses to our car and another $8000 for porch repairs. Thank goodness for insurance. This hill is often a danger to speeders who get spooked by its double curve. We are very concerned that any walker enjoying a pleasant evening stroll will get fatally hit or suffer severe injury. Every day we are surrounded by numerous dangers that we might not even be aware of. There are no guarantees for a Christian but I am very grateful to God thus far for His promise of protection. Throughout the years I am sure I have been able to avoid many other potential crises that Satan threw my way.

*But the Lord is faithful, and he will strengthen you
and protect you from the evil one.*
2 Thessalonians 3:3

● ● ● ● ● ● ● ●
A Musing

One day I was sitting out on our front porch and enjoying the afternoon sun. All of a sudden I heard a lot of squawking coming from quite a large group of birds in our neighbor's trees across the street. They were probably grackles who had spotted a cat down below. They were no doubt trying to protect their young. I saw the cat scoot out of the nearby bushes down the street. They immediately flew to the next tree to follow his path. What a great team effort in scaring their enemy off.

Paul, the apostle wrote a letter to his friends in the Ephesian church from his prison in Rome. He was always concerned about how people lived their Christian lives unitedly in Christ. He urged them to function as one body with each individual contributing their own special talents to the greater cause. Much can be accomplished in that process.

From him the whole body, joined and held together
by every supporting ligament, grows and builds itself
up in love, as each part does its work.
Ephesians 4:16

16. Negative and Positive Reputations

Starlings & Dandelions

Starlings, unfortunately, don't have the best reputation. They are very noisy when congregating as a group and very aggressive, often competing relentlessly with other birds over a desired nesting spot. Farmers who grow grapes and cherries are particularly not happy with these pests who will damage their crops. These blackbirds with yellow streaks on their backs, yellow beaks and orange legs and feet periodically visit our feeding platform. They only stay briefly as they prefer insects to seeds which is actually a good thing. I have seen them eating the red berries on the sumac bushes beside our driveway.

European starlings were introduced to North America from Europe in the late 1890s so that they could remind immigrants about the homeland they had left behind. One particular group released 60 of them into New York's Central Park. They wanted to bring over all the birds mentioned in William Shakespeare's plays. Today this bird population is approximately 200 million throughout our continent from coast to coast. Those introducers' plan worked very well!

The yellow dandelion is known as a pesky weed throughout many places in the world. It is a perennial that likes moist soil. A young pastor from Myanmar (Burma) visited us in 2011 to see what our life is like in Canada. When William saw a field of yellow he couldn't understand why we would want to get rid of them. The field or someone's lawn doesn't look very nice when the yellow heads turn to white round balls of seed that blow away in the wind. Did you know that the seeds can germinate up to nine years after being in the ground? They are extremely difficult to pull out as their roots go down deep. They seem to grow everywhere even through some paving we had done in our driveway. I was fighting with one in a crack in our front walkway one day and remembered that pouring boiling water on the weed works. It did the trick and is a very cheap solution if you are just dealing with a few at a time. People put the greens in a salad, make dandelion wine from the flower heads, use them as a medicinal herb or apply the milky substance from the stems as a mosquito repellent. Little children love to bring their moms a bouquet of these flowers that they have picked. This weed's reputation is not always bad.

Ellis, my father was also an immigrant like the starlings. He was born in Finland where he spoke Swedish and came to Canada in his 20s. Unlike the starlings or the dandelions he developed a good reputation in his family life, workplace, neighborhood and church where he loved playing his saxophone for many years. This hard working respected carpenter/builder could fix almost anything. He loved to be outside puttering around his home and keeping the yards immaculate. He believed that was part of being a great testimony for his Lord and was always annoyed when a Christian neighbor let dandelions take over their lawn. At age 95 he was up patching his roof and two years later he was caught climbing a ladder to trim tree branches. He loved studying his Bible and anything else he wanted to learn about right up until his death at age 99. He could have been a good overseer or deacon in a church but he was too quiet and reticent to let himself stand in that kind of a position; however he did set an example for others to follow. He could always be counted on when he made a commitment of any sort. That was my Dad!

If anyone sets his heart on being an overseer,
he desires a noble task. ... He must also have a good
reputation with outsiders...
I Timothy 3:1-7

● ● ● ● ● ● ● ●
A Musing

It is interesting to watch the various visitors to our seed station throughout the day. One minute there will be a red-winged blackbird, a black-capped chickadee, a cardinal and a cowbird all enjoying the food together. In a flash they could all be gone with the arrival of a blue jay, a sparrow, a dove plus any other specie that cares to join them. Surprisingly, all of these birds cooperate quite well together, except for the occasional ornery dove who likes to battle them all.

I don't do very well with any kind of conflict whether it be a disagreement with a relative, neighbor, co-worker, or even a fellow church member. It can be very upsetting. A list of positive characteristics that a person should strive for is found in Galatians 5:22-23, "But the fruit of the Spirit is love, joy, peace, forbearance, kindness, goodness, faithfulness, gentleness, self-control..." It seems to me that this is the kind of life God desires for each one of us. There is no place for "hatred, discord, jealousy, fits of rage, selfish ambition, dissensions" as recorded previously in verse 20 of that chapter.

How good and pleasant it is
when brothers live together in unity!
Psalm 133:1

17. Preparing for Change

Canada Geese & Sunflowers

Who tells Canada geese it's time to fly south to warmer climates in Mexico and the southern US? Weeks before they must be pumping up their strong bodies with extra food to be able to endure the long flight. These migratory birds fly over our property in the fall as they train for their flight patterns. One particular sunny day about a dozen landed on the roof of our house – that was noisy. We weren't quite sure what was happening with that exercise.

When we lived in Windsor we enjoyed visiting Jack Minor's bird sanctuary near Kingsville where thousands and thousands of these huge creatures have landed in his fields since 1904 before they take to the skies. These birds are the second largest waterfowl in North America. Average weight is 11-12 pounds and average age span is 10-25 years. The male gander has a low pitch "honk" sound while the female goose has a higher pitch "hink" call. They thoroughly enjoy life on our Credit River. It is marvelous how God has built within mechanisms for them to be able to prepare for and manage such change in their lives. Their "V" formation allows them to fly faster and longer and their care for each other when one gets sick or tired is a great example to us all.

Gary's favorite flower is the annual cheery sunflower which is native to the Americas. The sunflower will put a smile on anyone's face. In the 16th century the seeds were sent to Europe for cooking oil. Carleigh, our young granddaughter and Gary like to watch these very large plants develop and change over the summer. They need full sun and well drained moist soil with lots of mulch. They grow between 1.5 and 3.5 m (5–12 ft) high depending on the variety. The heads of young sunflowers follow the sun from east to west during the course of a day but mature yellow flower heads stay fixed towards the east. We have had to stake them up as they get very heavy. Carleigh helps Gary take the dry seeds out of its round base in the fall so that we can plant more flowers another year. You might be familiar with the Dutch painter, Vincent Van Gogh and his series of famous paintings, Sunflowers. He painted these in 1887 and 1888 while living in Paris.

In 1980 Gary became the founding pastor of a new church in St. Thomas where we lived. After a few years the congregation purchased land for a church building plus a senior citizen's complex. Many eagerly put their name on the waiting list but when they had actually been assigned a unit to rent and knew a move was forthcoming it was extremely difficult for these dear folk. These accumulators needed to make numerous decisions regarding getting rid of cherished items particularly if they owned a larger home than the residence they were moving into. I don't want my children's lives made more difficult as well when I move on to my home with God and so weekly I have to keep thinking about getting rid of stuff that is no longer usable.

No one likes change in his or her life but it is inevitable. However, there is nothing more exhilarating than observing a person become a child of God and mature thereafter within that new status. Life values become God-centred. We don't need to cling to our stuff for we can't take it with us to our final destination where no doubt the flowers will be bigger and better than the best of our sunflowers. Like the Canada geese, no baggage allowed.

> *Therefore, if anyone is in Christ, he is a new creation;*
> *the old has gone the new has come!*
> **2 Corinthians 5:17**

A Musing

Many can't remember the difference between annual versus perennial plants. Annual flowers generally bloom from the time you get them in the ground until frost arrives on the scene – all in one season. These bedding plants then die off. They need to be repurchased the following spring after their seeds have been helped to get started since our growing conditions are not perfect or long enough. They don't expand a whole lot in size and tend to be more costly in the long run. Perennial flowers, on the other hand, appear in the same spot of your garden every year and will bloom at specific times. The flowers usually last only a few weeks. Depending on the root system they can increase quite a bit from one year to the next; for example, sweet woodruff with its little white perfumy flowers in the spring tends to take over a large area but is easy to pull out. Without much difficulty you can split perennials and plant a patch of them elsewhere. In my opinion both kinds of plants have advantages and disadvantages. It's like comparing apples and oranges - we can enjoy them all.

Command those ... to put their hope in God who
richly provides us with everything for our enjoyment.
I Timothy 6:17

18. Looking On

Owls & Sedum

Every now and then when our bedroom window is open at night I hear the hoot of an owl who is probably sitting on our rooftop or in a spruce tree nearby. And that is all I know about the owls in Churchville. I have never seen one in broad daylight. Apparently we have 11 types of owls (including the Great Horned, Snowy, Screech and Short Eared) living in southern Ontario that are the "silent hunters of the night" usually looking for rodents. I am assuming the one I heard was the Great Horned owl since they are the most numerous in the Americas. All owls lay white eggs. I was surprised to learn that their wing span can spread up to five feet. How can they keep from hitting the tree branches as they soar through the darkness? To help with that they have exceptional night vision with their large round eyes and sensitive hearing. Some cultures associate this with wisdom. The ancient Greek goddess of wisdom, Athena, is often seen holding an owl. I like the old owl ditty:

There was an old owl
Who lived in an oak.
The more he saw,
The less he spoke.
The less he spoke,
The more he heard.
Why can't we be like that wise old bird.

I also like easy and the perennial sedum is one of the easiest plants to live with. During spring and summer it looks great beside other plants because of its interesting thick leaves that can withstand long periods of drought. The pale colored flowers begin to develop in late summer. They look like broccoli florets and will attract butterflies. They usually come in shades of pink and mauve which darken as the fall arrives. These plants seem to grow like a round ball from the inside out and don't take over the whole garden patch; they remain neat and tidy. When they get too big I just split them down the middle and move them to a new location where they will keep adding to their size. Like the owls this greenery just lives quietly in the background and watches the world around them. Come winter the dried flowers provide additional appeal.

When Solomon, David's son, became king we learn from I Kings 3 that he wanted to govern the Israelite people with justice. Since there were so many of them it was hard to count them all. That also meant lots of problems to handle. Solomon asked God for a "discerning heart to govern your people and to distinguish between right and wrong (verse 9)." God responded positively by declaring, "I will give you a wise and discerning heart, so that there will never have been anyone like you, nor will there ever be (verse 12)." Soon after he gave wise counsel to two women who had each born babies. Unfortunately the one had lain on her baby which died. They were arguing who was the real mother of the remaining live baby. I'll let you read the story to find out Solomon's solution. God has given my husband, Gary, a wise and analytical mind. I am amazed at the good advice he has given so many people who have rejected the advice and then subsequently said they were wrong not to follow it. Our society has become too skeptical but our all wise God is always there to see us through the next problem. We just have to ask.

For the eyes of the Lord range throughout the earth
to strengthen those whose hearts
are fully committed to him.
2 Chronicles 16:9

● ● ● ● ● ● ● ●

A Musing

Over and over again I realize how huge God's love is for us through the extreme variety He has created in the vast number of flowers and birds (all of nature as a matter of fact) for us to enjoy every day. I was surprised again this summer over the brilliant color of my tall purple phlox. The butterfly bush with its pretty lavender, brush-like flowers attracts the most interesting butterflies. Every fall I look forward to seeing the magnificent crimson-colored leaves of the sumac with their flower "bobs" growing beside our driveway. The freshly picked raspberries from the plants at the back of the barn are so much tastier than buying them from the grocery store. These are a result of bees pollinating the little white flowers earlier in the spring. God's system works.

For as high as the heavens are above the earth, so
great is his love for those who fear him.
Psalm 103:11

19. Knowing or Not Knowing

Orioles & Lungwort

For a few seconds one day Gary and I spotted a black-hooded, orange-breasted bird in the evergreens near our kitchen window. It was a Baltimore oriole.

This bird was named after an Englishman, Lord Baltimore, visiting Virginia in colonial times. He was so impressed with its coloring that he wanted his coat of arms to display similar colors. Females have a belly that is more yellow. As with many of the birds in our backyard, until I started writing this book I didn't know much about many of them like this beautiful songbird with its unique whistle. It has become one of North America's favorites. Orioles don't go for seeds as they mainly thrive on insects, fruit and nectar. I must put out a hummingbird feeder for them and the hummingbirds this summer. They love a juicy orange cut in half to peck at. They only remain in our area from May to early September and then return south to Central and South America. Unlike any other bird one of their most distinctive features is their ability to weave a pouch like nest from bits of grass, string, strips of bark etc. which hangs down from the end of a branch high up in a very tall deciduous tree. The nest is constructed over several days mostly by the female. It has to be very strong to withstand extremely blustery winds. So how do they know how to do that?

Do you know about lungwort? I didn't until I saw this ground cover with attractive silver dotted foliage blooming at the back of our property in the shade. My gardening expert next door came to my rescue once again. This plant originated in central Europe. Way back when, the leaves were thought to symbolize infected lungs and so this perennial herb was used to treat internal infections such as tuberculosis, asthma, coughs along with gastrointestinal and kidney problems. It is also used externally for eczema, hemorrhoids, wounds and burns. The flowers are bell-shaped, clustered and usually change from pink to blue as they age during the months of April and May. Once the flowers are gone the plants still look very attractive until the fall. They spread but are very easy to pull out. They are deer resistant which is a good thing in our village because of these animals that like to roam at night.

Sydney, Gary's dad, was known as a child evangelist when Gary was a youngster. He recalls the many Friday evenings he helped his dad load up their car with his home-made "electric sign" to accompany him to another church where Syd taught children Bible lessons with the use of this board. He was also very well known in his home church of Forward Baptist in Toronto, ON. He loved to help out so when the church moved into their new building he spent many an hour fixing one problem or another. This happened even more so after he received his gold watch upon retirement as a teacher from Bell Canada. Near the end of his life his heart wasn't working very well. One day he ran to catch a bus to visit a friend in the hospital. It proved too much for his heart and he died a few days later.

Syd had a great desire to let others know about His Lord's love for them. I'm finding it very interesting to learn more about bird and flower life around me and then spread that knowledge around to others; however it is more important that I let them know about what the Lord has done for them as my father-in-law tried to do in many different ways.

Give thanks to the Lord, call on his name;
make known among the nations what he has done.
Psalm 105:1

● ● ● ● ● ● ● ●
A Musing

I'm sure you have heard a cicada singing on a hot summer day but have you ever seen one of these "tree crickets?" (Just for your information, only male cicadas make their extremely loud sounds by contracting "tymbal" muscles on the sides of the abdomen that make a clicking noise. The inside of their abdomen is hollow so the sound is amplified.) There is so much wildlife hidden in our surrounding trees and bushes and that is why Gary and I decided to keep feeding birds at our seed station throughout the year. The free food draws them out so that we can see what they really look like. By watching them we can figure out their various habits and characteristics. By the way, some birds like to add cicadas to their diet.

It is always great to be in the "know." Knowledge is powerful, wouldn't you agree? But unfortunately as finite human beings we cannot know about all the hidden things that are going on in our world let alone understanding the mind of God. As His children one day we will when we go to live with Him. That will be exciting!

> *My purpose is that they may be encouraged in heart*
> *and united in love, so that they may have the full*
> *riches of complete understanding in order that they*
> *may know the mystery of God, namely Christ,*
> *in whom are hidden all the treasures*
> *of wisdom and knowledge.*
> ***Colossians 2:2-3***

20. Life & Death

House Wrens & Mock Orange

Everyone loves babies whether they be human or animal. New life is special. A few years ago we purchased a small two-storey wooden birdhouse at a Mennonite fair which had been made in a third world country. We hung it at the corner of our barn under the eaves. The following May we were excited to see a couple of migrant house wrens from the southern U.S. move in. These brown songbirds are very small (11-13 centimeters or 4-5 inches) and only weigh about 12 grams (0.42 oz). They will take over woodpecker holes to nest but also like man-made birdhouses. They mainly eat insects such as spiders and snails as well as butterfly larvae. Even though they are tiny in size wrens can get feisty and are known to destroy other birds' eggs by puncturing the eggshell. The couple will breed two to eight red-blotched cream-white eggs with the female incubating them for about 12–19 days. The male will bring her food. It is a good thing that the holes of our birdhouse are very small as one day when I went out to garden a grackle was perched on top. He was trying to snatch the eggs which they are prone to do. When the babies are born it takes another 15–19 days before they are ready to fly out on their own. They certainly can get noisy. We have now had two families living in our birdhouse and this fall when they leave for the sunny south again we must scrub it out with a weak bleach solution (one part chlorine bleach to nine parts warm water) to prevent disease from insects, feather mites, fungus or bacteria.

June comes along each year and my mock orange bush, a member of the hydrangea family and a native shrub in British Columbia, starts blooming at the front of our house where it thrives in the full sun. The white flowers with four petals form a cup to hold about two dozen yellow-tipped stamens. The name is derived from these flowers looking like those on orange and lemon trees at first glance. Another name used is Philadelphus after an ancient Greek king of Egypt, Ptolemy II Philadelphus. The flowers look very pretty in a wedding bouquet for a country bride. Our neighbor across the street has a beautiful mock orange tree that is probably over 12 feet tall. You can smell its sweet fragrance from a distance as you walk down the street. It is best to prune the branches after the blossoms have died along with thinning out any older dead branches. If you do it later in the year the floral display for the next year will be reduced. I like bringing some of these flowers in for a bouquet on my kitchen table but unfortunately they don't last very long as their life source has been cut off.

Everyone likes to talk about babies but no one likes to talk about death. We marvel at God's new creations with their fragile innocence and complete dependence on parents. Education is a key component from the womb to the tomb. A birth is generally joyful and exciting; whereas death is a very sad time of loss, questioning, remembering. Most look forward to the annual celebrations surrounding the birth of Jesus Christ but few want to hear about His death, burial and resurrection some thirty years later and what that means to every individual personally. The multitudes don't want to address what happens to their soul after death. They have a "wait and see" attitude. Others are following belief systems that are not trustworthy. The last book of the Bible, Revelation written by the apostle John, can be difficult to understand but there is so much encouragement for eternal life we can take from the first part of chapter 21. Unlike my dying mock orange blossoms, my life source is God and His Son, Jesus Christ forever and ever.

Now the dwelling of God is with men,
and he will live with them. They will be his people,
and God himself will be with them and be their God.
He will wipe every tear from their eyes. There will be
no more death ... I am the Alpha and the Omega,
the Beginning and the End. To him who is thirsty
I will give to drink without cost
from the spring of the water of life.
Revelation 21: 3-4, 6

● ● ● ● ● ● ● ●

A Musing

Communication in the bird world is amazing and intricate. Cornell University is known for its ornithology department and their website is excellent in helping you decipher bird noises. Another great URL to assist you in your "birding by ear" is www.birdjam.com. A robin can make 10 different sounds whereas a cardinal's repertoire is 16. Bird communication reveals various purposes such as singing, calling or alarming. The sounds can be one, two or three syllable phrases, often clear whistles or just raspy squeaks. A bird may sing more often at one time than at other times depending on the hour of the day, season, feeding, mating. Some can produce two different sounds at the same time because of their paired voice box structure. Many birds can mimic other birds or even human noises.

Human communication is also quite phenomenal. Can you keep up with the ever-growing list of tools the technological industry is creating day by day to help us connect and develop relationships with one another? Recently a friend was visiting Arizona and all of a sudden a sandstorm blew up near her hotel. Her friend immediately received a weather alert on her phone to run for cover.

God knew the importance of communication from day one. In the Old Testament we read He talked with Adam and Eve in the Garden of Eden (Genesis 3:9); He talked with Jacob at Bethel in the land of Canaan (Genesis 35:13); He talked with Gideon in Judges 6:17. In the New Testament we learn that God sent His Son Jesus to communicate with His chosen people at the beginning of the first century. The four Gospels are filled with conversations. God also provided man with His written Word, the Bible, authored by various men He inspired so that they would know what He wanted them to record.

But these are written that you may believe
that Jesus is the Christ, the Son of God and
that by believing you may have life in His name.
John 20:31

A Final Thought or Two

So what are some conclusions from my study on God's flowers and birds in my backyard? No matter the type of flower, I understand Jesus saying they do not "labor or spin." They are just there for our enjoyment in all their living splendor with their roots digging down deep. They grow from the inside out and spread themselves around. God provides the soil, the sun and the showers. They don't have a care in the world when all three provisions are there but they also don't have any control over their own existence.

On the other hand, the birds, even though God provides their food without their sowing or reaping of the seeds, still need to take the initiative to go after that food to sustain themselves and their offspring. They work hard come rain or shine. Mr. & Mrs. Cardinal landed on our feed station during an all day rain. This poor couple looked drenched in their soggy feathers with their crests lying flat on their heads. Birds don't procrastinate and will take some risk; however they don't worry or panic about it all unless they are being attacked. They do it!

Each month Gary and I host a luncheon in our home for our local pastoral association for our Baptist denomination. It seems these men with some wives who join in really enjoy coming together for the food and the fellowship. They need this time away, even for a few minutes, from the ongoing cares and worries of their church world. Often I am told they really appreciate my hostessing capabilities. By nature I would much prefer sitting quietly in a corner as I listen to others around me but I have learned the importance of this event. I get bothered when someone remarks that they don't have a certain gift or skill for a particular ministry. Sometimes in our developing Christianity we must dig down deep within ourselves to become what is beneficial to the whole. With much practice that can happen over time. You never know how God will spread yourself around to others in good ways.

Early one morning I needed to cut the long grass on our lawn before the rain started. First of all, however, it was necessary to have a talk with myself to get going on the job. Maybe it could wait for a few days after the much needed rain stopped. Maybe I would get struck by lightning if it turned stormy. It had already started to sprinkle and I would get soaked. You know the drill. Thank goodness, my procrastination didn't win out this time and I don't think I have ever had my lawn cut before 9:30 a.m. It took less time than our Canadian Women's Soccer team to earn their much coveted but unexpected Olympic Bronze medal at the London 2012 games that was happening at the same time. I came back into the house with a grin on my face and exclaimed to Gary, "I did it!" He asked, "You got the whole thing done?" I nodded my head and retorted, "Of course!" He replied sarcastically, "I should have known!" I did get a little soaked near the end (not sure if an electric lawn mower is a good thing to be used in the rain!) but in exchange the exercise has its rewards for an old lady like me.

I'm also glad I can say "I did it!" in regard to finishing this book. And then what will be my next great initiative? What will be yours? Jesus encouraged us to not sweat it whatever it is. He's the one in control if you let Him.

P.S. (You thought I was finished. Almost, but I had to tell you about another bird I just saw recently on our feeder. He was the size of a robin but his feathers were mottled beige and dark green. I have never seen one like him before. Interesting. I agree with my dad who believed that there was always something else to learn about no matter one's age.)

Consider This

by Sara Burton & Gayle Newton (2003 – based on Proverbs 6:6-8;
Luke 12:24-27; Psalm 107:43; Ecclesiastes 7:13)

Consider the ant.
Consider its ways
Consider this and be wise
God built into him a need to harvest and store
As He did for me and you.
Chorus:
Consider what God has done for you.
Consider the great love God has for you.
Consider the raven
All the birds of the air.
They don't plant or store their food.
God provides every thing they need.
Consider the lilies
All the flowers in the field.
Consider their beauty and be sure.
If God cared enough to dress the grass of the fields
He cares for me and you.

Appendix: The Flow of Life

by Wendy Carter (a Churchville resident)

As I look out my upstairs bedroom window, my eyes are searching for you in the distance. You are rather hard to see as the long flowing branches of the tall evergreens beside and beyond the little white cottage across the road are blocking most of my view. But I know you are there. You have been a comfort and an intrigue from the day my husband, Gary, and I moved into our 19th century home in late 2006. Our home is located in the historical village of Churchville, nestled between the two suburban cities of Mississauga and Brampton in Ontario. You are the winding Credit River that flows through this hamlet on your journey to Lake Ontario, just west of Toronto.

You were first named Rivière au Crédit by the French fur traders who bartered with the local native Mississauga Indians in the 1600s. Trading goods were provided in advance or on "credit" for furs that would be supplied the following spring by these Indians. In the early 1800s your river banks were settled by United Empire Loyalists who had been given parcels of crown land. And in 1815 this little village was founded by Amaziah Church who built a saw and grist mill right beside you. Others built a tannery, a slaughter house, a school house, churches, hotels etc. in the ensuing years. Many of these peoples' lives are remembered in the Churchville Cemetery on the hill.

If you could speak, what stories of nature and people would you tell about this interesting spot in your excursion? Seldom does a week go by that Gary does not walk the 200 yards to the bridge that crosses your watery path. He tries to imagine what you have seen over the last two hundred years and more.

Would you talk about the numerous differing species of wildlife that have survived because of your waters (1330 plants, 64 fish, 41 mammals, 5 turtles, 8 snakes, 17 amphibians, 244 birds)? You are well known for the yearly spawning of chinook salmon and rainbow trout. How many nights have you listened to the baying of wolves? How many deer have walked your shores? Were you able to see in the distance the night they smashed pumpkins with their hooves in our neighbor's field behind our house? How many beavers have you spied chomping down perfectly good trees along your banks for their dams? How many large, fragile, sprawling Manitoba Maple trees, known for living near your riverbed, have crashed to the ground in a wild rainstorm? How many Canadian geese have floated on your water before taking to the skies? Do you marvel at all the different kinds of colorful or unusual insects that flit about overhead each day in the warm weather or the nocturnal creatures that sound out their existence in the cool of the night?

Or would you talk about the yearly breakup of ice? You are probably quite amused by all the watchers who come to see how far up the banks you can toss huge, thick chunks of ice like cement. It really is amazing to see your ice break up in one day and disappear. Does it scare you when dynamite has to be used to break up ice jams from winters that have been extra severe? Were you impressed by the people who built the berms (earthen walls) in the backyards of the homes along your river side to keep out flood waters each spring?

Your collection of stories of people's lives down through the years must seem endless to you. It is just like the continual flow of water through the 1500 kilometer length of your body and tributaries that seems never-ending to us. Did you catch Amaziah Church's sense of adventure and freedom the day he began building the foundation of his 3-storey mill? He knew he could depend on you to turn his wheel to grind grain or transport pine logs for ship building on Lake Ontario.

Do you remember all the funeral processions that have flowed through the Churchville Cemetery? Amaziah Church who donated the land was the first to be buried there in 1831. Were you able to see the grief of the various mourners as they walked or arrived in their horse-drawn wagons or sleighs of old or modern-day automobiles, trucks and vans? The cemetery is filled with graves of all ages over these two hundred years; but it must have been particularly sad for those parents who lost so many infants due to sickness or accident. One of the largest funerals occurred in 1840 for the local blacksmith, William Hardy. He had the reputation of being able to hammer all four shoes on a horse in one minute.

Did your tears of laughter flow downstream the day the fiery William Lyon Mackenzie was forced to flee across to your other bank? Being a strong supporter, Orange Church, Amaziah's son, had allowed Mr. Mackenzie to speak out for his Reform cause for Upper Canada. The second storey of his father's mill served as a public hall. Apparently the Tories opposed what he was saying and a mini-riot broke out. Eight Tories and seven Reformers landed in your waters clubbing each other. In 1834 William Lyon Mackenzie, journalist and politician, did become the first Mayor of Toronto and his grandson, William Lyon Mackenzie King was Canada's Prime Minister during World War II.

Did you watch the people faithfully gathering each Sunday at their choice of church – Episcopal, Wesleyan Methodist, Anglican – to gain strength for the hardships that would arise during the week? Can you recall the day that Joseph Smith, founder and prophet of the Mormon religion, visiting from the U.S., preached at the schoolhouse in the summer of 1837? The Churchville "branch" or "stake" had become quite active with many members being baptized in your waters - often very frigid – to show the seriousness of their faith. In a few short years, most of these people emigrated, bravely traveling by covered wagon to Sault Lake City, Utah to their new "Zion." Today there are no churches in this residential hamlet. One year a group of well-meaning Sikhs purchased a home on a huge lot to create a place of worship. Unfortunately, with much angst from the neighborhood, they could not make a "go" of it and the property has been sold again.

How many have relied on your water to put out the numerous fires that have occurred in the village through the years? Often businesses were not rebuilt; owners just decided to move elsewhere. In the early 1950s Churchville did get its own fire station and engine which has now been shut down. Did you admire the firemen who faithfully headed out to an emergency whether it was during the light of day or the dark of night? I'm sure you heard the fire engine roaring up the hill as it tried to gain speed. The firemen washed down their fire engine with so much pride every Sunday morning. Were you startled by the screaming siren one fall when the fire engine raced over your bridge to a historical home nearby that was engulfed in flames? The home with all its memories and memorabilia was owned by a widower in his 80s who had lived there all his life. What a loss for this gentleman, his family and the community! Months before, a heritage barn on Creditdale farm was destroyed by another blaze. Maybe arson was the cause for both of these horrific fires and others.

Were you excited to have families relax and have fun picnicking along your shores each summer weekend the ice cream parlor was open a half century ago? And how about the skaters and hockey players who enjoy the man-made rink in the Churchville park on a sunny, cold day each winter?

You have been immersed in change all through these civilized years. Were you snubbed by the development of the railway system in the 1850s? Your waterway was no longer needed as much. This resulted in many relocating to the Village of Brampton, a short distance away, which later formed a town and then a city. Today it has grown to be one of the largest urban centers in Canada. Churchville, even though flourishing at the time of its inception, remains a village of about 100 homes today. Do you hear the whistle of the freight train in the distance each afternoon as the train journeys south to Streetsville?

Your path was even somewhat redirected when local road development started occurring about ten years ago. A major city highway crossed over your course just to the south of the village. Were you offended by this progress as the villagers have been? Did you want things to stay the same as nature planned?

But the flow of progress didn't stop there. Brand-new neighborhoods with contemporary, immaculate homes have emerged surrounding Churchville. It's as if Churchville has become a basin below with you traveling through its middle. To continue to develop and provide modern convenience, a huge 2-year sewer project was built in the village. This resulted in the creation of a gigantic tunnel 60 feet below the earth's surface to transport all the sewage south. How have you fared with all the extra dust, noise and traffic? I am sorry for the pollution and garbage clutter that invades your space day by day. Maybe the "Canoe the Credit" in June of each year will draw attention for the need of our citizens to clean up their act for nature's sake.

All I can say is thank you for continuing to contribute to the comfort and well-being of us villagers! You have left behind rich soil for excellent flower and vegetable gardens and fruit farms. You have also provided a peacefulness and serenity that our friends immediately sense and love when they visit our home or stroll through the village. Their bones are less weary when they leave; they are happy for the pleasant experience. May you continue to flow through our lives and those not yet born as only you know how!

Please Note: Information for this article has been gathered from several websites – Wikipedia, Credit Valley Conversation, City of Brampton – as well as the research from archival documents in the Peel Heritage Complex, Brampton.

Wendy Elizabeth Carter

97

Made in the USA
Charleston, SC
24 September 2014